A Little Book of House Blessings

A Little Book of House Blessings

Compiled by
Peter Watkins

CANTERBURY
PRESS
Norwich

First published in 2007 by the Canterbury Press Norwich
(a publishing imprint of Hymns Ancient & Modern
Limited, a registered charity)
9–17 St Alban's Place, London N1 0NX

www.scm-canterburypress.co.uk

British Library Cataloguing in Publication data

A catalogue record for this book is available
from the British Library

ISBN 978-1-85311-829-6

Typeset by Regent Typesetting, London
Printed and bound by
M P G Books, Bodmin, Cornwall

Contents

INTRODUCTION

'Blessings abound where e'er He reigns', so the hymn goes. For whatever we hold most precious and sacred we pray for blessing. We desire that what is most important to us is indeed something approved of by God. We pray that all our endeavours find divine favour. That if we build a ship we want it blessed. If we harvest produce we want our fields to be blessed. If we fish we even need the very seas to be blessed. We offer solemnly our services of worship and conclude them with a blessing. We bring our beloved children to the font to be blessed. We bless each other – even when we sneeze. Blessings indeed do abound in countless situations.

And we acknowledge that we need a blessing. This little book is about the need for a blessing. Arthur Miller, once the husband of Marilyn Monroe, a worldwide icon of beauty who met a tragic death, simply said of her: 'She needed a blessing.' We can certainly do without a curse. The vibrations of certain people and places can seem malignant. Some are gifted in detecting sad or evil atmospheres attached to certain localities and buildings. The haunting of some houses can be more than unpleasant: it can be terrifying.

Few things are more precious to us than our homes. They also need a blessing. At the memorable concert in Carnegie Hall on 26 January 1975 Barbara Cook sang 'A House Is Not a Home'. The melody was by Burt Bacharach and the lyrics by Hal David. She sang of the way in which a house becomes a home through the blessing of love. Part of that blessing in a family home is the love between parents and children. Psalm 127 speaks of the virtue of God's blessing: 'Except the Lord build the house'. It also declares that 'children are our heritage and gift that cometh of the Lord'. Blessed is the man that 'hath his quiver full of them'. When, long ago, the Countess of Winchilsea wrote her poem 'The Petition for an Absolute Retreat', her prayer was for a sweet and quiet home, but with someone in it to love.

> ... since Heaven has shown
> It is not good to be alone.

PART ONE
THERE'S NO PLACE LIKE HOME

Home sweet home

Except the Lord build the house,
 they labour in vain that build it:
except the Lord keep the city,
 the watchman waketh but in vain.

Psalm 127.1, AV

God gives the desolate a home to dwell in.

Psalm 68.6, NRSV

Mid pleasures and palaces though we may roam,
 Be it ever so humble, there's no place like
home.

J. H. Payne, The Maid of Milan

Charity begins at home.
>> *Traditional*

East, west, home's best.
>> *Traditional*

The strength of a nation is derived
from the integrity of its house.
>> *Confucius*

In love of home, the love of country has its rise.
>> *Charles Dickens*

The snail, which everywhere doth roam,
Carrying his own house still, still is at home.
>> *John Donne*

⁹’Tis sweet to hear the watch-dog's honest bark
    Bay deep-mouth'd welcome as we draw near
home;
’Tis sweet to know there is an eye will mark
    Our coming, and look brighter when we come.

George Gordon, Lord Byron

He is happiest, be he king or peasant,
    who finds peace in his home.

Johann Wolfgang von Goethe

Stay, stay at home and rest;
    Home-keeping hearts are happiest.

Henry Wadsworth Longfellow

Happy the man whose wish and care
    A few paternal acres bound,
Content to breathe his native air,
In his own ground.

Alexander Pope

In I Capture the Castle *by Dodie Smith, Cassandra Mortmain describes a perfectly happy day in terms of a certain homecoming:*

. . . All day long I had a sense of great ease and spaciousness. And my happiness had a strange, remembered quality as though I had lived it before. Oh, how can I recapture it – that utterly right, homecoming sense of recognition? It seems to me now that the whole day was like an avenue leading to a home I had loved once but forgotten, the memory of which was coming back so dimly, so gradually, as I wandered along, that only when my home at last lay before me did I cry: 'Now I know why I have been happy!'

HOME IS . . .

O how amiable are thy dwellings:
   thou Lord of hosts!
My soul hath a desire and longing to enter into the
courts of the Lord:
   my heart and my flesh rejoice in the living God.
Yea, the sparrow hath found her an house, and the
swallow a nest where she may lay her young:
   even thy altars, O Lord of hosts, my King and my
   God.
Blessed are they that dwell in thy house:
   they will be alway praising thee.

Psalm 84.1–4, BCP

What a word home is! To think that God has made the world so that you have only to be born in a certain place, and live long enough in it to get at the secret of it, and henceforth that place is to you a home with all the wonderful meaning of the word.

George MacDonald

To Adam, paradise was home. To the good among his descendants, home is paradise.

Augustus Hare

Home is where the heart is.

Pliny the Elder

Home is the place where, when you have to go there,
They have to take you in.

Robert Frost

A man travels the world over in search of what he needs and returns home to find it.

George Moore, The Brook Kerith

Home is not where you live but where they
understand you.

Christian Morgenstern

Where Thou art – that is home.

Emily Dickinson

Lord, Thou hast given me a cell
    Wherein to dwell;
A little house, whose humble Roof
    Is weather-proof;
Under the spars of which I lie
    Both soft, and dry;
Where Thou my chamber for to ward
    Hast set a Guard
Of harmless thoughts, to watch and keep
    Me, while I sleep.
Low is my porch, as is my Fate,
    Both void of state;
And yet the threshold of my door
    Is worn by th' poor,
Who thither come, and freely get
    Good words, or meat:
Like as my Parlour, so my Hall

And Kitchen's small:
A little Buttery, and therein
   A little Bin,
Which keeps my little loaf of Bread
   Unchipped, unflead;
Some brittle sticks of Thorn or Briar
   Make me a fire,
Close by whose living coal I sit,
   And glow like it.
Lord, I confess too, when I dine,
   The Pulse* is Thine,
And all those other Bits, that be
   There placed by Thee;
The Worts, the Purslain, and the Mess
   Of watercress,
Which of Thy kindness Thou hast sent;
   And my content
Makes those, and my beloved Beet,
   To be more sweet.
'Tis Thou that crown'st my glittering Hearth
   With guiltless mirth;
And giv'st me Wassail Bowls to drink,
   Spiced to the brink.
Lord, 'tis Thy plenty-dropping hand,
   That soils my land:
And giv'st me, for my Bushel sown,

Twice ten for one:
Thou mak'st my teeming Hen to lay
    Her egg each day:
Besides my healthful Ewes to bear
    Me twins each year:
The while the conduits of my Kine
    Run Cream, (for Wine).
All these, and better Thou dost send
    Me, to this end,
That I should render, for my part,
    A thankful heart;
Which, fired with incense, I resign,
    As wholly Thine;
But the acceptance, that must be,
    My Christ, by Thee.

*Robert Herrick, 'A Thanksgiving
                    to God for his House'*

*beans, peas, etc.

LONGING FOR HOME

*The painful yearning for home has been expressed
often and all over the world, from the misery of
children at boarding school to the lament of exiles
far from their native land.*

By the waters of Babylon we sat down and wept:
  when we remembered thee, O Sion.
As for our harps, we hanged them up:
  upon the trees that are therein.
For they that led us away captive required of us then
a song, and melody in our heaviness:
  Sing us one of the songs of Sion.
How shall we sing the Lord's song:
  in a strange land?
If I forget thee, O Jerusalem:
  let my right hand forget her cunning.

Psalm 137.1–5, BCP

Jesus said, 'Foxes have holes, and birds of the air have nests; but the Son of Man has nowhere to lay his head.'

Matthew 8.20, NRSV

My heart's in the Highlands, my heart is not here;
My heart's in the Highlands a-chasing the deer;
Chasing the wild deer, and following the roe,
My heart's in the Highlands, wherever I go.

Robert Burns

In 'Londonderry Air' the singer, in a hauntingly sorrow-ful melody, yearns to see Derry Vale again:

Oh tarrying years, fly faster ever faster,
I long to see the vale beloved so well,
I long to know that I am not forgotten,
And there at home in peace to dwell.

Peace and rest at length have come,
All the day's long toil is past;
And each heart is whispering
'Home, home at last!'

Thomas Hood, 'Home at Last'

Weep no more, my lady;
   Oh, weep no more today!
We will sing one song for the old Kentucky home,
For the old Kentucky home, far away.

Stephen Foster

In Wind in the Willows *by Kenneth Grahame, written in 1908, Rat and Mole go on a great expedition. Mole at length is attacked by a violent bout of homesickness. A strong theme of this classic novel is the love of home. There is the pleasant riverside dwelling of Rat, the magnificent hall of Toad, and the large and rambling house of Badger. Mole longs for his own small home in the chapter entitled* Dulce Domun *(Sweet Home).*

The Rat, astonished and dismayed at the violence of Mole's paroxysm of grief, did not dare to speak for a while. At last he said, very quietly and sympathetically, 'What is it, old fellow? Whatever can be the matter? Tell us your trouble, and let me see what I can do.'

Poor Mole found it difficult to get any words out between the upheavals of his chest that followed one upon another so quickly and held back speech and choked it as it came. 'I know it's a – shabby, dingy little place,' he sobbed forth at last, brokenly: 'not like – your cosy quarters – or Toad's beautiful hall – or Badger's great house – but it was my own little home – and I was fond of it – and I went away and forgot all about it – and then I smelt it suddenly – on the road, when I called and you wouldn't listen, Rat – and everything came back to me with a rush – and I *wanted* it! – O dear, O dear! – and when you *wouldn't* turn back, Ratty – and I had to leave it, though I was smelling it all the time – I thought my heart would break. We might have just gone and had one look at it, Ratty – only one look – it was close by – but you wouldn't turn back, Ratty, you wouldn't turn back! O dear, O dear!'

Recollection brought fresh waves of sorrow, and sobs again took full charge of him, preventing further speech.

The Rat stared straight in front of him, saying nothing, only patting Mole gently on the shoulder. After a time he muttered gloomily, 'I see it all now! What a *pig* I have been! A pig – that's me! Just a pig – a plain pig!'

SHELTER AND PROTECTION

If you make the Most High your dwelling place, even the Lord, your refuge, then shall no harm befall you, no disasters come near your dwelling place.

For he will give his angels charge of you, to guard you in all your ways.

Psalm 91.9, 11, NRSV

The fruit of righteousness shall be peace. My people will live in peaceful dwelling places, in secure homes, in undisturbed places of rest.

Isaiah 32.17–18, NRSV

Be our shelter, Lord, when we are at home,
our companion while we are away,
and our welcome guest when we return,
and at the last receive us into the dwelling place
you have prepared for us in your Father's house,
where you live for ever and ever. Amen.

Catholic Household Blessings and Prayers

Visit we beseech Thee, O Lord, this dwelling,
and drive far from it all the snares of the enemy.
Let Thy holy angels dwell in it, to preserve us in peace,
and may Thy blessing be upon us evermore;
through our Lord Jesus Christ.
Amen.

The Office of Compline, BCP

A man's house is his castle.
Sir Edward Coke

Saint Francis and Saint Benedict
Bless thys House from Wicked Wight,
From the Nightmare and the Goblin that is hight!
Goodfellow Robin keepe it
From all evil Sprites, Fayries, Wezles, Bats and
   Ferryts,
From curfew Time till the next Prime!

Traditional

Wight –
   hight –
Prime –

The sacred Three
My fortress be
Encircling me
Come and be round
My hearth, my home.
   A Hebridean prayer
      for protection

God shield the house, the fire, the cows,
And all who sleep herein.
This night, preserve all those I love
From violence and harm.

Save us from our enemies
May Mother Mary's Son
Protect us while we take our rest
This night, and nights to come.

A Celtic Prayer

God banish from your house
The fly, the roach, the mouse

That riots in the walls
Until the plaster falls;

Admonish from your door
The hypocrite and liar;

No shy, soft, tigrish fear
Permit upon your stair,

Nor agents of your doubt,
God drive them whistling out.

Stanley Kunitz, 'Benediction'

Peace comes not by establishing a calm outward setting so much as by inwardly surrendering to whatever the setting.

Hubert von Zeller

May nothing evil cross this door,
  And may ill fortune never pry
About these windows; may the roar
  And rain go by.

Strengthened by faith, these rafters will
Withstand the batt'ring of the storm;
This hearth, though all the world grow chill,
  Will keep us warm.

Peace shall walk softly through these rooms,
Touching our lips with holy wine,
Till ev'ry casual corner blooms
  Into a shrine.

Laughter shall drown the raucous shout;
And, though these shelt'ring walls are thin,
May they be strong to keep hate out
  And hold love in.

Louis Untermeyer, This Singing World

HOSPITALITY

Now as they went on their way, he entered a certain village, where a woman named Martha welcomed him [Jesus] into her home.

The Gospel of Luke 10.38, NRSV

So they drew near to the village to which they were going. He [Jesus] appeared to be going further, but they constrained him saying, 'Stay with us, for it is toward evening and the day is far spent.' So he went in to stay with them.

Luke 24.28–29, NRSV

In that day, says the Lord of hosts, every one of you will invite his neighbour under his vine and under his fig tree.

Zechariah 3.10, NRSV

Be not forgetful to entertain strangers: for thereby some have entertained angels unawares.

The Epistle to the Hebrews 13.2, AV

O God, protect our going out and coming in.
Let us share the hospitality of this home with
all who visit us,
that those who enter here may know your love and
peace.

Catholic Household Blessings and Prayers

O king of stars!
Whether my house be dark or bright,
Never shall it be closed against any one,
Lest Christ close His house against me.

If there be a guest in your house
And you conceal aught from him,
'Tis not the guest that will be without it,
But Jesus, Mary's Son.

Traditional Celtic

A guest never forgets the host who has treated him kindly.

Homer

Hail Guest, we know not whom thou art.
If friend, we greet thee hand and heart.
If stranger, such no longer be.
If foe, our love will conquer thee.

Early Welsh

Come in the evening, come in the morning,
Come when expected, come without warning;
Thousands of welcomes you'll find here before you,
And the oftener you come, the more we'll adore you.

Traditional Irish

The blessing of God upon this house . . .
With plenty of food and plenty of drink,
With plenty of beds and plenty of ale,
With much riches and much cheer,
With many kin and length of life,
ever upon it.

A Hebridean blessing

Part Two
House blessings

BLESSINGS FOR A HOME

The blessing of a home traditionally involves a pro-cession from one room to another with an appro-priate prayer said in each room. Sometimes the Eucharist is also celebrated in the house. The cere-mony is usually conducted to mark the new occu-pation of a house. It is customary for some to have their home blessed each year after one of the great festivals. Others may desire a house blessing after a disruption in the family or a bereavement, after any stressful or tragic event. The form and wording of the ceremony is created and adapted to fit the par-ticular circumstances and participants.

The Eastern Orthodox Church celebrates a sac-rament to mark the laying of a corner-stone or foundation stone of a new house.

There follows a selection of general blessings for a home, and particular blessings for individual rooms.

The Lord shall be mindful of us, and he shall bless
us:
  even he shall bless the house of Israel, he shall bless
  the house of Aaron.

Psalm 115.12, BCP

May the Lord give you increase,
  you and your children!
May you be blessed by the Lord,
  who made heaven and earth!

Psalm 115.14–15, NRSV

Pax intrantibus,
  Salus exeuntibus.
Benedicto habitantibus.

Peace to those who enter,
Health to those who depart.
Blessings to those who dwell within.

A Latin Blessing

Dios bendiga cada Rincon de esta casa.

God bless every corner of this house.

A Spanish Blessing

Whom God loves, his house is sweet to him.

Miguel de Cervantes, Don Quixote

God our Father, bless and hallow this house, that it may be
a haven for those in need,
a place of gladness and goodwill,
Where each person is good to and good for all the
    others, and
where all that is true and lovely is appreciated.
May the books on the shelves bring wisdom;
may the pictures on the walls inspire a sense of
    beauty; and
may the music throughout bring joy to everyone.

Peter Watkins

Bless this house, O Lord we pray;
Make it safe by night and day;
Bless these walls so firm and stout,
Keeping want and trouble out.

Bless the roof and chimneys tall,
Let thy peace lie over all;
Bless this door, that it may prove
Ever open to joy and love.

Bless these windows shining bright,
Letting in God's heavenly light;
Bless the hearth a-blazing there,
With smoke ascending like a prayer.

Bless the folk who dwell within,
Keep them pure and free from sin;
Bless us all that we may be
Fit O Lord to dwell with thee.

Bless us all that we one day
May dwell O Lord with thee, we pray.

Helen Taylor wrote the lyric and Mary Brahe composed the music of this song. It was published in 1927 and was first widely heard when the Irish tenor John McCormack included it as a highlight of his repertoire. It has since been recorded and sung countless times.

Touch the lintel and touch the wall,
Nothing but blessing here befall!
Bless the candle that stands by itself,
Bless the books on the mantle shelf,
Bless the hearth and the light it sheds,
Bless the pillow for tired heads.
Those who tarry here, let them know
A threefold blessing before they go:-
Sleep for weariness – peace for sorrow –
Faith in yesterday and tomorrow.
Those who go from here let them bear
The blessing of hope wherever they fare.
Lintel and window, sill and wall,
Nothing but good this place befall.

Traditional

Bless the four corners of this house,
And be ye lintel blest.
Bless ye hearth and bless ye board
And bless each place of rest.

Bless each door that opens wide
To strangers as to kin.
And bless each crystal window pane
That lets the sunshine in.

And bless ye roof tree* overhead
And every sturdy wall –
The Peace of man, the Peace of God,
The Peace of Love on all.

Traditional

*Another name for a ridgepole.

God bless the house
From site to stay,
From beam to wall,
From end to end,
From ridge to floor,
From balk* to roof-tree,
From found to summit.

Celtic Traditional

*A balk was a beam or rafter.

May the roof above never fall in,
May we below never fall out.

Traditional Irish prayer

Hail King! Hail King!
Blessed is he; Blessed is he;
Bless this house and all that it contains,
From rafter and stone and beam,
Deliver to God from pole to cover,
Be the healing of men therein.
Hail King! Hail King!
Blessed is he; Blessed is he;
Without beginning, without ending,
From everlasting to eternity
Every generation for aye,
Ho! Hi! Let there be joy!

Traditional Celtic Blessing

God's peace to me, peace of mankind,
And Saint Columba's peace, the kind,
Mild Mary's peace, a loving thing,
And peace of Christ the tender King,
The peace of Christ the tender King.

Be on each window, on each door,
Each cranny-light upon the floor,
On house four corners may it fall,
And on my bed's four corners all,
Upon my bed's four corners all.

Upon each thing mine eye doth see,
Upon each food that enters me,
Upon my body of the earth,
And on my soul of heavenly birth,
Upon my body of the earth
Upon my soul of heavenly birth.

A Celtic Blessing

A Christmas House Blessing

God bless your house this Holy night,
    And all within it:

God bless the candle that you light,
    To midnight's minute;

The board at which you break your bread,
    The cup you drink of:

And as you raise it, the unsaid
    Name that you think of:

The warming fire, the bed of rest,
    The ringing laughter:

These things and all things else be blest
    From floor to rafter.

This Holy night, from dark to light,
    Even more than other:

And if you have no house tonight,
    God bless you, brother.

Eleanor Farjeon

THE DOOR

Surely the Lord is in this place! This is none other than the house of God, and this is the gate of heaven.

The Book of Genesis 28.16–17, NRSV

The Lord shall preserve thy going out and thy coming in from this time forth, and even for evermore.

Psalm 121.8, AV

Whatever house you enter, first say, 'Peace to this house.'

The Gospel of Matthew 10.5, NRSV

'Behold, I stand at the door and knock; if any one hears my voice and opens the door, I will come in to him and eat with him, and he with me.'

Revelation 3.20, NRSV

The artist Holman Hunt was inspired by this verse of the Bible to paint his famous picture 'The Light of the World' which hangs in St Paul's Cathedral, London. It depicts Jesus knocking on a stoutly closed door, overgrown with weeds, as night is falling. This is a door that is rarely, if ever, opened.

O God,
    make the door of this house
wide enough to receive all who need human love and
    fellowship; and
narrow enough to shut out all envy, pride and strife.
Make its threshold smooth enough to be no stumbling-
    block to children,
nor to straying feet,
but rugged and strong enough to turn back the power
    of evil.
God make the door of this house
the gateway to thine eternal kingdom.

Lancelot Andrewes

May joy and peace surround you,
and contentment latch your door.
May your trouble be less,
and your blessings be more,
and nothing but happiness
come through your front door.

An Irish Blessing

Not many sounds in life, and I include all urban
and all rural sounds, exceed in interest a knock
at the door.

Charles Lamb

Any guest ... should be received just as we would
receive Christ himself, because he promised that
on the last day he will say, 'I was a stranger and you
welcomed me.'

The Rule of St Benedict

THE KITCHEN AND DINING ROOM

Thou dost cause the grass to grow for the cattle,
and plants for man to cultivate,
that he may bring forth food from the earth,
and wine to gladden the heart of man,
oil to make his face shine,
and bread to strengthen man's heart.

Psalm 104.14–15, NRSV

Better is a dry morsel with quiet
than a house full of feasting with strife.

Proverbs 17.1, NRSV

Grant, O Lord, that all who work in this kitchen
may know that in serving others they are
  serving thee.
In all the busyness and bustle of this room
may they possess their souls in peace.
May they be thankful for their daily bread
and always mindful of the needs of others.
Eat thy bread with joy,
And drink thy wine with a merry heart.

Source unknown

THE KITCHEN AS A PLACE OF PRAYER

*Nicholas Herman was born in Lorraine about 1605.
In 1649 he entered a Discalced Carmelite monastery
in Paris, taking the name of Brother Lawrence. The
Abbé de Beaufort met him and took notes of their
conversations. He also collected Lawrence's letters
and wrote a memoir of him after his death in 1691.
The collections were published in two volumes. A
selection of his prayers and letters was published in
1934 under the title* La Pratique de la presence de Dieu
and later translated into English under the title The
Practice of the Presence of God.

*Brother Lawrence worked for fifteen years in the
kitchens of the monastery and then in the cobbler's
workshop. Everywhere was a place of prayer for him.
Here are two quotations from* The Practice of the
Presence of God.

The time of business does not differ from the time of prayer; and in the noise and clatter of my kitchen, while several persons are at the same time calling for different things, I possess God in as great tranquillity as if I were upon my knees at the Blessed Sacrament.

We can do little things for God: I turn the cake that is frying on the pan, for love of him; and that done, if there is nothing else to call me, I prostrate myself in worship before him who has given me grace to work; afterwards I rise happier than a king.

We saw a stranger yesterday.
    We put food in the eating place,
Drink in the drinking place,
Music in the listening place,
And with the sacred name of the triune God
He blessed us and our house,
Our cattle and our dear ones.
As the lark says in her song:
'Often, often, often, goes Christ
In the stranger's guise'.

A Celtic Rune of Hospitality

I would like to have the men of Heaven
In my own house:
With vats of good cheer
Laid out for them.

I would like to have the three Marys,
Their fame is so great.
I would like people
From every corner of Heaven.

I would like them to be cheerful
In their drinking,
I would like to have Jesus too
Here amongst them.

I would like a great lake of beer
For the King of Kings,
I would like to be watching Heaven's family
Drinking it through all eternity.

St Brigid of Kildare

For food to eat,
   for friends to share it,
for health to enjoy it,
and for those who prepare it,
thanks be to God.

Anonymous

Be present at our table, Lord,
   Be here and everywhere ador'd.
These creatures bless and grant that we
May feast in Paradise with thee.

Anonymous

Bless, O Lord, before we dine,
   Each dish of food, each glass of wine,
And Bless our hearts that we may be
Aware of what we owe to Thee.

Anonymous

Bless my kitchen, Lord,
I love its every nook
And bless me as I do my work
Wash pots and pans and cook.

May the meals that I prepare
Be seasoned from above
With blessing and thy grace
But most of all thy love.

As we partake of earthly food,
The table thou hast spread,
We'll not forget to thank thee, Lord,
For all our daily bread.

So bless my kitchen, Lord,
And those who enter in.
May they find naught but joy and peace
And happiness therein.

Anonymous

THE LIVING ROOM

Behold, how good and joyful a thing it is:
brethren, to dwell in unity!

Psalm 133. 1, AV

Good Lord, unite those who gather around the
hearth of this room in true friendship. May they
form a bond of forbearance and tolerance and a chorus
of laughter and affectionate conversation.

Peter Watkins

The ornament of a house is the friends who frequent
it.

Ralph Waldo Emerson

Few are born to do the great work of the world, but the work that all can do is to make a small home circle brighter and better.

George Eliot

The beauty of this house is order.
The blessing of this house is contentment.
The glory of this house is hospitality.
The crown of this house is godliness.

A fireplace motto

The fire in the hearth is symbolically the centre of the family circle. This was reflected in a lyric by Lena Guilbert Ford of a song with a melody composed by Ivor Novello. It became immensely popular during the Great War of 1914–18. It expressed a longing for the family circle to be complete.

Keep the home fires burning
while your hearts are yearning.
Though your lads are far away
they dream of home.
There's a silver lining
through the dark cloud shining.
Turn the dark clouds inside out
till the boys come home.

THE STUDY, STUDIO, WORKROOM OR OFFICE

The Lord is my light . . .
Psalm 27.1, AV

The Latin of these opening words of Psalm 27, Dominus Illuminatio Mea, *is the motto of Oxford University. It has been in use since at least the second half of the sixteenth century, and it appears on the University's arms.*

For thou art my lamp, O Lord: and the Lord will lighten my darkness.
The Second Book of Samuel 22.29, AV

Creating God, sculptor of land and sea, be present with those who share in their work the joy and beauty of thy creation. Amen.

Source unknown

O Lord God, the true Light that lightens everyone who comes into the world, enlighten those who study in this place that they may gain a knowledge of thy truth and will and learn to love it and do it. Amen.

Peter Watkins

Laborare est orare

To work is to pray

A monastic rule

It is not only prayer that gives God glory but work. Smiting on an anvil, sawing a beam, whitewashing a wall, driving horses, sweeping, scouring, everything gives God some glory if being in his grace you do it as your duty. To go to communion worthily gives God great glory, but to take food in thankfulness and temperance gives him glory too. To lift up the hands in prayer gives God glory, but a man with a dungfork in his hand, a woman with a slop-pail, give him glory too. He is so great that all things give him glory if you mean they should. So then, my brethren, live.

Gerard Manley Hopkins

Study as though you were to live forever. Live as though you were to die today.

Anonymous

O Christ the Master Carpenter,
   Who at the last, through wood and nails,
   purchased our whole salvation,
Wield well your tools in the workshop of your world,
So that we who come rough-hewn to your bench
may here be fashioned to a truer beauty of your hand.
For your own name's sake. Amen.

George Macleod, Founder of the Iona Community

Teach me, my God and King,
  in all things thee to see;
and what I do in anything
to do it as for thee.

A man that looks on glass,
on it may stay his eye;
or, if he pleaseth, through it pass,
and then the heaven espy.

All may of thee partake;
nothing can be so mean
which, with this tincture, for thy sake,
will not grow bright and clean.

A servant with this clause
makes drudgery divine;
who sweeps a room, as for thy laws,
makes that and th'action fine.

This is the famous stone
that turneth all to gold;
for that which God doth touch and own
cannot for less be told.

George Herbert, 'The Elixir'

Sunrise marks the hour for toil to begin, but in our souls, Lord, prepare a dwelling for the day that will never end.

Ephraem the Syrian

Almighty God, Giver of Wisdom, without whose help resolutions are vain, without whose blessing study is ineffectual, enable me, if it be thy will, to attain such knowledge as may qualify me to direct the doubtful, and instruct the ignorant, to prevent wrongs, and terminate contentions; and grant that I may use that knowledge, which I shall attain, to thy glory and my own salvation, for Jesus Christ's sake. Amen.

Samuel Johnson

THE BEDROOM

I will lay me down in peace, and take my rest:
For it is thou, Lord, only, that makest me dwell in safety.

Psalm 4.9, BCP

You have made us for yourself, O Lord, and our hearts are restless until they rest in you.

St Augustine

Sweet is the sleep of labourers . . .

The Book of Ecclesiastes 5.12, NRSV

Lord God, our heavenly Father, you neither
slumber nor sleep.
Bless the bedrooms of this house
and guard with your continued watchfulness
all who take rest within these walls,
that refreshed by the gift of sleep
they may awake to serve you with joy.

God of life and love,
thou art the true rest of thy people.
We are restless until we find rest in thee;
give rest and refreshment to thy servants.

Be present, O merciful God,
and protect us through the silent hours of this night,
so that we who are wearied by the changes and
    chances of this fleeting world,
may repose upon thy eternal changelessness;
through Jesus Christ our Lord.

Look down, O Lord, from thy heavenly throne,
illuminate the darkness of this night with thy celestial
    brightness,
and from the sons of light banish the deeds of
    darkness;
through Jesus Christ our Lord.
Amen.

Sleep after toil, port after stormy seas,
Ease after war, death after life does greatly
please.

Edmund Spenser

Blessed art Thou, O Lord our God, who makes the
bands of sleep to fall upon mine eyes, and slumber
upon mine eyelids. May it be Thy will, O Lord my
God, to suffer me to lie down in peace and to let me
rise up again in peace. Let not my thoughts trouble
me, nor evil dreams, nor evil fancies, but let my rest be
perfect before Thee. Amen.

Hebrew Prayer-book

My Christ! My Christ! My shield, my encircler,
Each day, each night, each light, each dark:
My Christ! My Christ! My shield, my encircler,
Each day, each night, each light, each dark.

Be near me, uphold me, my treasure, my triumph,
In my lying, in my standing, in my watching, in my
sleeping.

A Hebridean encompassing prayer

Glory to thee, my God, this night
for all the blessings of the light;
Keep me, O keep me, King of kings,
beneath thy own almighty wings.

Thomas Ken

A morning prayer

O God, who broughtest me from the rest of last
night
Unto the joyous light of this day,
Be Thou bringing me from the new light of this day
Unto the guiding light of eternity.

A Celtic invocation

New every morning is the love
our waking and uprising prove;
through sleep and darkness safely brought,
restored to life and power and thought.

John Keble

A CHILD'S ROOM

Lo; children and the fruit of the womb:
  are an heritage and gift that cometh of the Lord.
Like as the arrows in the hand of the giant:
  even so are the young children.
Happy is the man that hath his quiver full of them . . .

Psalm 127.4–6(a), BCP

Then little children were being brought to him in
order that he might lay his hands on them and
pray. The disciples spoke sternly to those who brought
them; but Jesus said, 'Let the little children come to
me, and do not stop them; for it is to such as these that
the kingdom of heaven belongs.' And he laid his hands
on them and went on his way.

The Gospel of Matthew 19.13–15, NRSV

Jesus said, 'Truly I say to you, whoever does not
receive the kingdom of God like a child shall not
enter it.'

The Gospel of Mark 10.15, NRSV

Almighty God our heavenly Father,
whose blessed Son didst share at Nazareth the
   life of an earthly home,
bless all the children who shall live in this house,
and grant wisdom and understanding to all who have
   the care of them,
that they may grow up to love and serve thee in word
   and deed. Amen.

BCP

O God in Heaven, whose loving plan
   ordained for us our parents' care,
and from the time our life began
the shelter of a home to share;
Our Father, on the homes we love,
send down Thy blessing from above. Amen.

Source unknown

[58]

Strength of character may be acquired at work, but beauty of character is learned at home. There the affections are trained. There the gentle life reaches us, the true heaven life. In one word, the family circle is the supreme conductor of Christianity.

Henry Drummond

Children have more need of models than of critics.

Joseph Joubert

Jesus, tender Shepherd, hear me,
  Bless thy little lamb tonight,
Through the darkness be thou near me,
Keep me safe till morning light.

Through this day thy hand has led me,
And I thank thee for thy care.
Thou has clothed me, warmed and fed me,
Listen to my evening prayer.

Let my sins be all forgiven,
Bless the friends I love so well;
Take me, when I die, to heaven,
Happy there with thee to dwell.

Mary D. Duncan

THE BATHROOM

Who shall ascend the hill of the Lord? And who shall stand in his holy place? Those who have clean hands and pure hearts, who do not lift up their souls to what is false and do not swear deceitfully. They will receive blessing from the Lord and vindication from the God of their salvation.

Psalm 24.3–5, NRSV

Have mercy on me, O God, according to thy steadfast love; wash me and I shall be whiter than snow . . . Create in me a clean heart and put a new and right spirit within me.

Psalm 51.1, 7, 10, NRSV

He [Jesus] riseth from supper, and laid aside his garments;
And took a towel, and girded himself. After that he poured water into a basin, and began to wash the disciples feet, and to wipe them with the towel wherewith he was girded.

John 13.4–5, AV

Blessed art Thou, Lord of heaven and earth;
Thou hast created us in wisdom and love;
Refresh us in body and spirit, and keep us in such
Health as we might serve thee best.

Adapted from Catholic Household Blessings
and Prayers

Creating breath of live,
Give health of body and wholeness of being
To those who use this room.

Adapted from Occasional Celebrations of the
Anglican Church of Canada

Cleanliness is next to godliness.

Hebrew proverb, quoted by
John Wesley in a sermon

THE GARDEN

The Lord God planted a garden in Eden, in the east, and there he put the man whom he had formed.

The Book of Genesis 2.8, NRSV

The Lord will guide you continually, and satisfy your needs in parched places . . . and you shall be like a watered garden, like a spring of water, whose waters never fail.

Isaiah 58.11, NRSV

O thou, who art the source of all life and hast made us stewards of the earth:
prosper those who dwell here in their care of soil and
    plants.
May the knowledge of thy presence grow
as they see the growth of their garden. Amen.

Peter Watkins

THE GARDEN

God Almighty first planted a garden; and, indeed,
it is the purest of human pleasures.

Francis Bacon

The Lord God planted a garden
    In the first white days of the world,
And he set there an angel warden
  In a garden of light enfurled.

So near to the peace of Heaven,
  That the hawk might nest with the wren,
For there in the cool of the even
  God walked with the first of men.

The kiss of the sun for pardon,
  The song of the birds for mirth –
One is nearer God's heart in a garden
  Than anywhere else on earth.

Dorothy Francis Gurney

The best place to seek God is in a garden.

George Bernard Shaw

Who plants a garden, plants happiness.

Chinese proverb

A garden is a lovesome thing, God wot!
  Rose plot,
  Fringed pool,
Ferned grot –
  The veriest school
  Of peace; and yet the fool
Contends that God is not –
Not God! in gardens! when the eve is cool?
  Nay but I have a sign;
  'Tis very sure God walks in mine.

Thomas Edward Brown

God made rainy days so gardeners could get the housework done.

Anonymous

Part Three
Homeward bound

HOMEWARD BOUND

Lord, thou hast been our dwelling place in all generations.

Psalm 90.1, BCP

Jesus said, 'In my Father's house are many mansions: if it were not so, I would have told you. I go to prepare a place for you.'

The Gospel of John 14.2, AV

You are only visitors here; your real home is in heaven.

1 Peter 2.11, The Message: The Bible in Contemporary Language, *Eugene Peterson*

Bring us, O Lord God, at our last awakening
into the house and gate of heaven,
to enter into that gate and dwell in that house,
where there shall be no darkness nor dazzling, but
   one equal light;
no noise nor silence, but one equal music;
no fears nor hopes, but one equal possession;
no ends nor beginnings, but one equal eternity;
in the habitations of thy glory and dominion,
world without end.

A prayer adapted from a sermon of John Donne

My soul's desire is to see the face of God, and to
rest in his house.

St Columba

SOURCES AND
ACKNOWLEDGEMENTS

I am grateful to the Revd Dr Mark Powell for several sug-
gestions and for bringing my attention to *Catholic Household Blessings and Prayers*, from which three titles are either
quoted or adapted. Adaptations have also been made from
Occasional Celebrations of the Anglican Church of Canada
and *Pastoral Offices for Prayers*.

Eleanor Farjeon, 1951, 'A Christmas House Blessing', in
Silver-Sand and Snow, Michael Joseph.

Pastoral Offices for Prayers, The Book of Common Prayer,
the rights of which are vested in the Crown, are reproduced
by permission of the Crown's Patentee, Cambridge University
Press.

Stanley Kunitz, 2000, 'Benediction', in The Collected Poems.
Copyright © 2000 by Stanley Kunitz. Used by permission of
W. W. Norton & Company, Inc.

Eugene Peterson, *The Message: The Bible in Contemporary
Language*, Navpress Publishing Group, 2002.

Dodie Smith, 2003, *I Capture the Castle*, St Martin's Griffin.

United States Catholic Conference, 1988, *Catholic Household Blessings and Prayers*, United Stated Conference of Catholic Bishops.

Louis Untermeyer, 1923, 'This Singing World', in *This Singing World*, Harcourt Inc.

Abbreviations:

AV
Authorized Version of the Bible (The King James Bible), the rights in which are vested in the Crown. Extracts are reproduced by permission of the Crown's Patentee, Cambridge University Press.

BCP
The Book of Common Prayer, the rights in which are vested in the Crown. Extracts are reproduced by permission of the Crown's Patentee, Cambridge University Press.

NRSV
Revised Standard Version of the Bible © 1989 Division of Christian Education of the National Council of the Churches of Christ in the United States of America.